EXTRAOR-BEE-NARY

Extraordinary Facts About Bees

An Educational Book About Honey Bees
With Illustrations for Children

seven puppies
PRESS

SPECIAL BONUS!

Want This Bonus Book for Free?

Get FREE unlimited access to it
and all of my new books
by joining the Fan Base!

EXTRAOR-BEE-NARY

seven puppies PRESS

26 MORE Extraordinary Facts About Bees

SCAN WITH
YOUR CAMERA
TO JOIN!

seven puppies
PRESS

ISBN 978-1-955626-02-6 (Paperback)
ISBN 978-1-955626-03-3 (Harcover)
ISBN 978-1-955626-04-0 (eBook)

Three types of honey bees live in every hive: a queen, worker bees, and drones.

A queen can lay up to 2,000 eggs in a single day!

All worker bees are females.
Male bees are called drones, and they
do not have a stinger.

Honey bees are everywhere.
In fact, the only place you wouldn't find
a honey bee is Antarctica.

Honey bees are social insects so they live
in large groups.
These groups are called "colonies".

Honey bees go through four life cycle stages:
egg, larva, pupa, and adult.

Bees build a hive out of honeycombs.

A single hexagonal shape within the honeycomb is called a cell, and it is made of wax.

Bees have five eyes.
Why do they need 5 eyes?

The two large eyes on the sides of their heads
are called "compound" eyes.
These compound eyes have many tiny lenses for see-
ing patterns and shapes.

The three small eyes in the top of their heads
are called "Ocelli", and they detect light and color,
but not shapes.

Older bees teach younger bees how to make honey.

Bees eat nectar and pollen from flowers.
Nectar is a sugary liquid that plants make.
Pollen is used by plants to produce fruits,
and it makes you sneeze.

Bees have long tongues, shaped like a straw,
to suck nectar out of flowers.

Worker bees waggle dance to show other bees where the nectar is.

In one trip, a honey bee
will collect nectar
from 50 to 100 flowers.

Honey bees can fly at a speed
up to 20 miles per hour.
Many humans cannot outrun
a honey bee at full speed.

A worker bee can carry a quantity of pollen or nectar equivalent to 80% of her body weight.

Bees navigate
using the Sun's position.

What if the weather is bad,
and they can't see the Sun?

Bees can see sunlight even
if the weather is bad because
their eyes are sensitive
to polarized light.

Those 5 eyes come in handy!

Honey bees make their buzzing sound by beating their wings 200 times per second.

Every year a single hive can produce
60 to 100 pounds of honey.

Beekeepers are honey farmers.
They keep bees in hives or boxes and collect
the bee honey.

Beekeepers only harvest
extra honey produced by the bees.

Honey bees
are the only insects
that produce food
consumed by humans.

Honey is a magical food
that lasts forever!

In their lifetime, worker bees will fly the distance of one and a half times around the Earth. That's more than 40,000 miles!

One ounce of honey can fuel a bee's flight around the world.

Bees interpret dark colors as natural predators. Remember, they use their Ocelli, on the top of their heads, to see light and color.

Watch out for bees if you are wearing bright clothes. The bees might mistake you for a flower.

Beekeepers wear white suits to avoid attracting the bees.

Bees can't see the color red.
To a bee, red looks black.

Honey bees don't sleep.
Instead, they spend their nights motionless,
like a statue.

They are saving their energy
for the next day's nectar hunt.

In winter, honey bees eat the honey they collected during the warmer months.

Some bees become "heater bees" in winter and vibrate their bodies to keep the hive warm.

Bees are extremely clean.

They bathe themselves frequently to protect the colony from viruses.

Bees pollinate numerous plants eaten by humans.

They also help the growth of trees, flowers,
and other plants, which serve as food for other species.

Bees are an important part of keeping
our environment clean and healthy.

thank you

for learning about honey bees!

RESOURCES

Beepods."101 Fun BEE Facts About Bees and Beekeeping" Accessed May 18, 2021.
https://www.beepods.com/101-fun-bee-facts-about-bees-and-beekeeping

NatureMapping Program. "Honey Bee" Accessed May 18, 2021.
http://naturemappingfoundation.org/natmap/facts/honey_bee_k6.html

The National Wildlife Federation. "Bees" Accessed May 18, 2021.
https://www.nwf.org/Educational-Resources/Wildlife-Guide/Invertebrates/Bees

eLife. "The cuticular hydrocarbon profiles of honey bee workers develop via a socially-modulated innate process" Accessed May 18, 2021.
https://elifesciences.org/articles/41855

Savannah Bee Company. "What is Honeycomb?" Accessed May 18, 2021.
https://savannahbee.com/blog/what-is-honeycomb

Beecasso Live Bee Removal. "All about the eyes!" Accessed May 18, 2021.
http://www.beecassolivebeeremoval.com/blog/2021/4/5/all-about-the-eyes

Ontario Beekeepers' Association. "Neat Facts About Bees" Accessed May 18, 2021.
https://www.ontariohoney.ca/kids-zone/bee-facts

RVC Outdoor Destinations. "20 Fun Facts About Honey Bees" Accessed May 18, 2021.
https://rvcoutdoors.com/20-fun-facts-about-honey-bees/

Swansons Nursery. "Honeybee Fun Facts" Accessed May 18, 2021.
https://www.swansonsnursery.com/honeybee-facts

Smithsonian Magazine. "The Science Behind Honey's Eternal Shelf Life" Accessed May 18, 2021.
https://www.smithsonianmag.com/science-nature/the-science-behind-honeys-eternal-shelf-life-1218690/

EarthSky. "Can bees see colors we can't?" Accessed May 18, 2021.
https://earthsky.org/earth/can-bees-see-colors-we-cant

Aquaponics and Earth. "Facts about Bees and Honey" Accessed May 18, 2021.
https://www.aquaponicsandearth.org/2009/08/facts-about-bees-and-honey/

PETA. "Small but Powerful—Here's the ONE Thing You Can Do to Help Bees" Accessed May 18, 2021.
https://www.peta.org/features/facts-about-bees/